FUN FACTS

Ripley's

Believe It or Not!®

Kids

& SILLY STORIES

RIPLEY
PUBLISHING

Publisher Anne Marshall

Editorial Director Rebecca Miles
Project Editor Charlotte Howell
Editorial Assistant Dominic Lill
Additional Text James Proud
Factchecker Alex Bazlinton

Art Director Sam South
Senior Designer Michelle Foster
Design Rocket Design (East Anglia) Ltd
Reprographics Juice Creative Ltd

Published by Ripley Publishing 2014
Ripley Publishing, Suite 188, 7576 Kingspointe Parkway
Orlando, Florida, 32819, USA

10 9 8 7 6 5 4 3 2 1

ISBN 978-1-60991-118-8

Library of Congress Control Number: 2014939814

Manufactured in China
in June/2014
1st printing

WARNING
Some of the stunts and activities in this book are undertaken
by experts and should not be attempted by anyone without
adequate training and supervision.

PUBLISHER'S NOTE
While every effort has been made to verify the accuracy
of the entries in this book, the Publishers cannot be held
responsible for any errors contained in the work. They
would be glad to receive any information from readers.

WHEEE!

FUN FACTS

Ripley's Believe It or Not!®

Kids

& SILLY STORIES

THE BIG ONE!

Who? Me?!

RIPLEY
PUBLISHING
a Jim Pattison Company

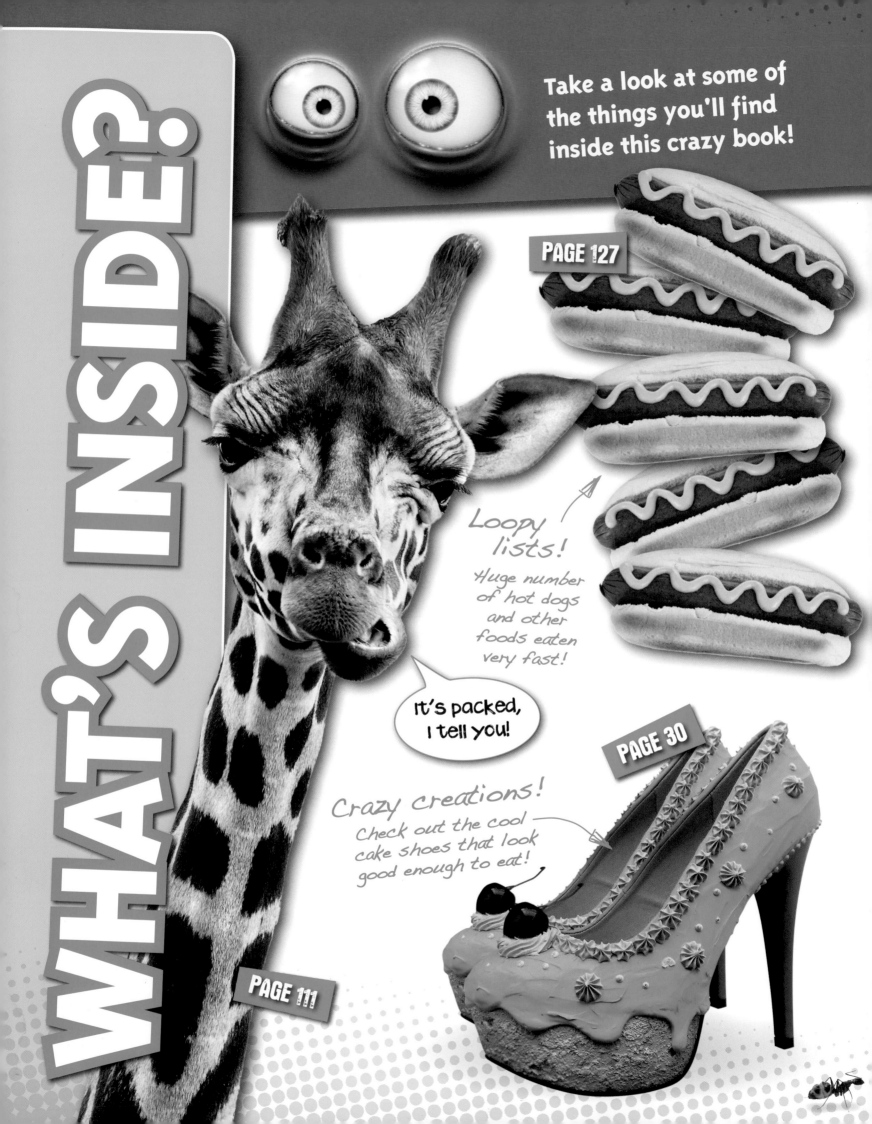

WHAT'S INSIDE?

PAGE 127

Take a look at some of the things you'll find inside this crazy book!

Loopy lists!
Huge number of hot dogs and other foods eaten very fast!

It's packed, I tell you!

Crazy creations!
Check out the cool cake shoes that look good enough to eat!

PAGE 30

PAGE 111

CHECK THIS OUT!

PAGE 81

They look tasty!

Silly stories! Meet the tortoises who love dressing up!

PAGE 56

Unbelievable facts... Believe It or Not!

PAGE 112

PAGE 49

AND WAY TOO MUCH FUN...

You're my princess!

where's the sugar?

PAGE 28

5

THINGS THAT FELL FROM THE SKY

WOAH!

MEAT

Lumps of meat fell from a clear blue sky in Olympian Springs, Kentucky, on March 3, 1876.

FISH

Hundreds of small white fish fell from the sky over the desert town of Lajamanu in Australia in February 2010.

Weeeee!

MAGGOTS

A mass of inch-long maggots came down in a heavy storm at Acapulco, Mexico, on October 5, 1968.

A shower of peaches fell from the sky onto a building site in Shreveport, Louisiana, on July 12, 1961.

PEACHES

HEADS

Hundreds of golf balls fell over Punta Gorda, Florida, on September 3, 1969.

GOLF BALLS

Spiders fell from the sky in Salta Province, Argentina, on April 6, 2007.

SPIDERS

TEAR JERKERS

Sea turtles drink salty seawater all their lives. They don't need all of its salt so they cry some of it out in their very **salty tears.**

Crocodiles lose salt through their tongues.

Seawater has so much salt in it that if you drink it, it would just make you very thirsty!

Seagulls drink seawater— they get rid of the unwanted salt in water that **trickles out** through their nose.

Aitchoo!

1 This yellow-spotted river turtle in the Amazon rainforest is surrounded by butterflies that have come to drink its tears.

Turtles have been around for 215 million years!

Keep still.

Gerroff!

2 It is very difficult to find salt in the rainforest, so the butterflies flutter around the turtles' heads to drink their salty tears.

3 If no turtles are around, the butterflies will get their salt from animal pee or sweaty humans!

Bees also drink turtle tears!

FUNNY FOODS

You'd be in for a surprise if you tried sucking up a strand of this spaghetti. It's really ice cream pushed through a spaghetti maker, with strawberry sauce on top, made by German chef Dario Fontanella.

A four-year-old boy in China wasn't too keen on getting up in the mornings, until his mom started to make his breakfast into a cute picture, like this one, every day.

BAGS OF FUN!

Every morning U.S. artist David LaFerriere brightens up his kids' packed lunches by drawing a picture on their sandwich bags. With 2,000 drawings so far, he plans to continue his daily doodles until his sons go to college.

THINGS YOU CAN'T DO IN SPACE

CRY
The tears just stick to your face!

BURP
Weightlessness in space turns any burps into vomit.

THINGS YOU SHOULDN'T TAKE INTO SPACE

SALT AND PEPPER
They would float and could get stuck in an astronaut's eyes and nose. Liquid salt and pepper are used instead.

FARTS
The bad smell stays in the space capsule for too long as there is nowhere for the gas to escape!

THINGS YOU CAN DO IN SPACE

PLAY STAR WARS
In 2007, a genuine light saber used in the Star Wars movies traveled into space onboard the space shuttle.

VOTE
American astronauts can vote in Earth elections from the space station.

TAKE A BATH

Astronauts clean themselves in a watertight shower that sucks away the dirty water.

TASTE

Astronauts lose their sense of taste and smell in space—so they like extra spicy food.

SLEEP IN A BED

Astronauts zip themselves into sleeping bags attached to the walls of the spacecraft so they don't float around.

A SPARE SET OF CLOTHES

Water on a spaceship is too precious for doing laundry.

A COLD

A sneeze floats around for far too long in a spacecraft and its germs have nowhere to go. This could lead to all of the astronauts getting sick.

STUFFED ANIMALS

They smell really bad after time in space.

BREAD

Crumbs could float away and damage equipment.

CARRY THE OLYMPIC TORCH

Two astronauts once carried the Olympic Torch on a spacewalk.

ORDER PIZZA

Pizza Hut delivered a salami pizza in a rocket to a Russian astronaut on the space station.

DRINK YOUR PEE

The space station recycles astronaut urine into water they can drink.

Ant-astic Strength!

Tiny weaver ants can hold onto objects, such as these pencils, that are hundreds of times heavier than their own bodies—that's like you carrying a whale!

The tiny moss mite is the strongest creature on Earth! It can hold 1,180 times its own weight, which is like a human lifting up a jumbo jet.

The froghopper bug can leap 100 times its own length!

Tigers can carry prey weighing half a ton—that's twice their own body weight—up a tree.

An African elephant is strong enough to carry over 100 humans at once— if they could all fit on its back!

If you were as strong as a rhinoceros beetle you could...

walk a mile with a car on your head!

LITTLE ZOOKEEPER

Charlie Parker the wildlife ranger is only four years old! He has grown up at the Ballarat Wildlife Park in Victoria, Australia, with snakes, frogs, and alligators.

SLIMY

Playing with frogs!

Question time...

Q What is your favorite animal?

A The Philippines crocodile. [This is a very rare croc we met at Melbourne Zoo—Charlie's mom.]

Q Are there any animals you are afraid of?

A The Taipan snake—it's very poisonous!

Q What is the biggest animal you've ever held?

A Baby, the Burmese python.

Q What do you like best about animals?

A I like all their different colors.

HEAVY

Charlie with Baby,
a 13-foot-long
Burmese python.

TOOTHY

Holding Gump, the
baby alligator.

EXTREME WEATHER

Tornado winds can spin at 300 mph and travel at 70 mph.

The wettest place in the world is a village in India called Mawsynram, which gets 40 feet of rainfall every year!

You can't make snowballs at the South Pole —the snow is too dry!

In 1934, a gust of wind on Mount Washington, New Hampshire, was measured at 231 mph.

A hailstone measuring 7 inches in diameter—almost as big as a bowling ball—fell in Nebraska in June 2003.

Lightning strikes actually travel from the ground upward, not from the sky downward!

East Antarctica is the coldest place on Earth. In 2010, the temperature dropped to −135.8°F.

The driest place in the world is the Atacama Desert in Chile. In 1971, rain fell for the first time in 400 years.

Around 6,000 bolts of lightning strike the Earth each minute!

In 1877, a New York newspaper reported that alligators fell from the sky in South Carolina!

BETTER TOGETHER

Crowd record breakers

1,110 Santa's elves

867 Supermen

Hmm, I don't belong here!

GET SOME CLOTHES ON!

Stop staring!

Naked mole rats are also sometimes known as sand puppies.

They don't feel pain on their skin.

This weird pink creature is a naked mole rat. It lives in dark underground burrows in East Africa, digging tunnels with its big teeth and feeling its way using its whiskers.

They can live for up to 31 years.

Their burrows can have up to 3 miles of tunnels.

They live in groups of up to 300 mole rats, all with their own jobs. Only one of the mole rats—the queen—has babies.

Raw carrots are STILL ALIVE when you eat them!

ZIP IT!

Japanese artist Kitagawa Jun creates giant 3-D zippers, such as this one laid across a pond. He makes the zany super-sized zippers from wood and metallic paint.

Every three minutes someone in the world reports seeing a UFO.

There's one!

Bees can count up to FOUR.

BEAST BUDDIES

Here's a furry feel-good story. This monkey in Thailand was rescued after a dog attack, and now lives with his gentle rabbit friend, Toby.

Brock the baby otter and Bumble Bee the badger cub became best friends at their wildlife center in Somerset, U.K.

Australian Dalmatian dog Zoe made friends with an orphaned black-and-white lamb. The lamb soon began to think he was a dog and slept in Zoe's kennel.

This baby monkey hitched a ride on a lion cub while playing with some baby tigers at a tiger park in China.

Over at Noah's Ark Farm near Bristol, U.K., Gerald the giraffe and Eddie the goat have buddied up. They look out for each other in the Africa enclosure, which they share with a bunch of zebras.

27

Are ants see-thru?

...yes, some are!

Dr. Mohamed Babu fed ants dyed sugar water and their insides changed color! Their favorite colors seemed to be yellow and green.

FOOT FOOD

Fashion designer Chris Campbell, from Florida, makes footwear that looks like fabulous food. The yummy decorations on his cake-style shoes aren't real, though. You can look at them, and wear them, but you can't lunch on them!

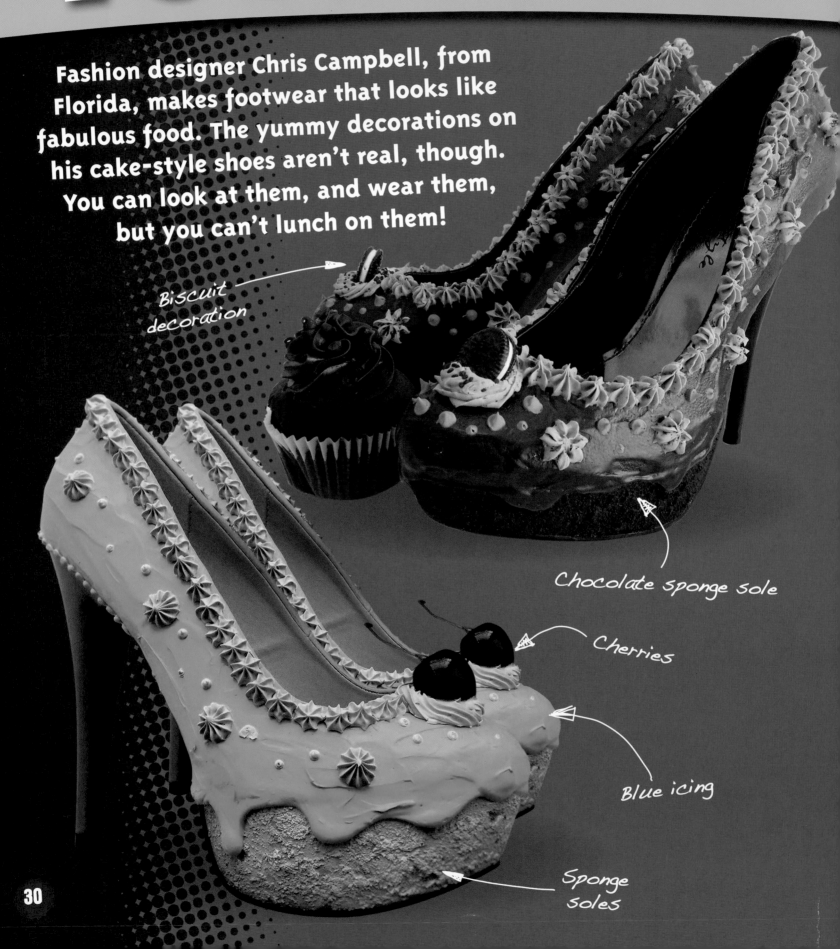

Biscuit decoration

Chocolate sponge sole

Cherries

Blue icing

Sponge soles

Yum, chocolate sauce and sprinkles!

More cherries

Piped icing

Gingerbread biscuit

BEE-WEAR!

Dang, I can't move!

She Ping was covered in more than 460,000 bees! The bee suit weighed over 100 pounds and he "wore" it for 15 minutes.

Snakes never stop growing.

Unlike people, who shrink when they get older!

Animals that lay eggs don't have **belly buttons.**

This includes fish, crocodiles, turtles, and birds.

When you blush, the lining of your stomach turns RED.

White peacock

White peacocks have no colors in their feathers, so when the males show off their fine tail feathers, they look like lovely lace fans.

CRAZY COLORS

Moor frog

Bright pink dragon millipedes are found in Southeast Asia. Their color warns predators of the poison in their body.

Dragon millipede

Male moor frogs turn bright blue when they are trying to find a mate. They do this so they can tell the difference between male and female frogs.

Mwanza flat-headed rock agama

Male lizards in this African species have crazy coloring that makes them look just like Spider-Man!

White Bengal tiger

White Bengal tigers are incredibly rare. They don't have the red and yellow pigments (natural colors) in their body that produce a tiger's usual orange fur.

Bright pink slug

Giant pink slugs come out to feed at night on Mount Kaputar in New South Wales, Australia. They grow up to eight inches long!

G'DAY!

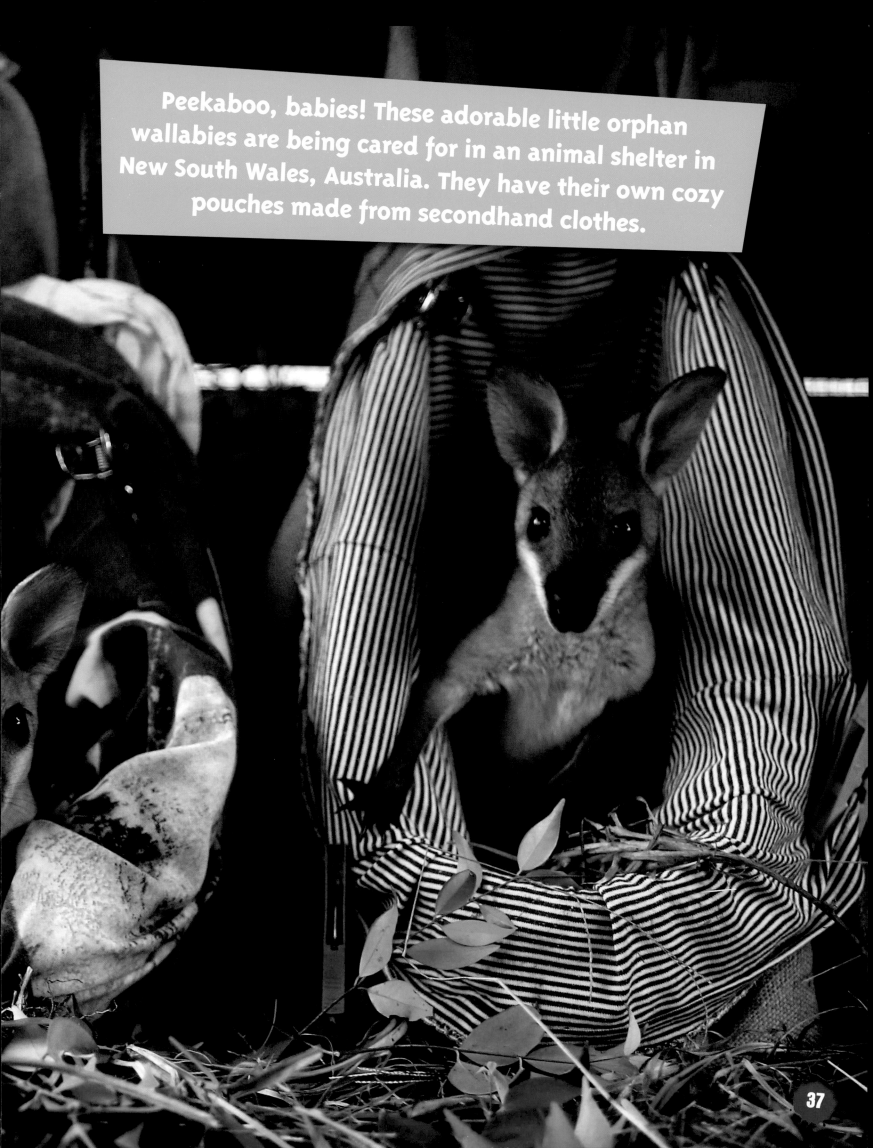

Peekaboo, babies! These adorable little orphan wallabies are being cared for in an animal shelter in New South Wales, Australia. They have their own cozy pouches made from secondhand clothes.

BALLOON MAN

Jeff Wright from Cleveland, Ohio, takes balloon twisting to a whole new level. He transforms himself into famous characters and superheroes, using up to 500 balloons for each amazing costume.

BUZZ LIGHTYEAR

To infinity, and beyond!

MARIO

38

Question time...

Q How long have you worked with balloons?

A I started twisting balloons at college, in 2006. I found out quickly that it was a great way to make people smile and make some money. Two years later I made my first costume.

Q How long does it take to make one costume?

A If things go well, I can make a full body costume in 8 hours. If I have to experiment with some tricky designs, it can stretch over a few days. My favorite piece, Buzz Lightyear, took me 10 hours.

Q How do you get in and out of the costumes?

A My costumes are made out of several pieces with my body acting as the skeleton to hold them all together. It's not *too* difficult to get in and out of the costumes, but it's always a good idea to go to the bathroom before putting them on!

IRON MAN

I'm bursting with grrr!

MONSTER

MINIONS!

39

BE AFRAID!

A phobia is an extreme fear of something, and every phobia has a name.

POGONOPHOBIA IS THE FEAR OF **BEARDS**

Parthenophobia is the fear of GIRLS

Coulrophobia is the fear of CLOWNS

Clinophobia IS THE FEAR OF GOING TO BED

Scoleciphobia is the fear of **Worms**

Ambulophobia is the fear of WALKING

Anthophobia IS THE FEAR OF **FLOWERS**

Koumpounophobia is the fear of **buttons**

HIPPOPOTOMONSTROSESQUIPPEDALIOPHOBIA
is the fear of LONG WORDS

ZOOPHOBIA
is the fear of ANIMALS

Tonsurephobia
is the fear of haircuts

TUROPHOBIA
is the fear of CHEESE

Triskaidekaphobia
Number 13

OMBROPHOBIA
is the fear of RAIN

AILUROPHOBIA
is the fear of CATS

WACKY RACERS!

This motorized dining table travels at an incredible 113 mph! It was created by Perry Watkins, from England, who can be seen driving from beneath the turkey in the middle of the "car."

Move those candles, I can't see where I'm going!

GRRR...

This customized big cat car from Singapore is a roaring success. It's striped like a tiger and it has terrifying teeth, too!

SLOSH!

This two-seater toilet car, built by Dave Hersch from Lakewood, Colorado, can hit speeds of 30 mph! Dave and his ten-year-old son, Miles, ride it around their local neighborhood.

This cool car, named Rex Rabbit, won a prize at the Houston Art Car Parade in Texas, where the world's wackiest cars go on parade.

This Volkswagen Beetle has been turned into Tori the Tortoise by Zoran Krstic in Australia.

43

Dinosaurs had no **eyelashes.**

Tasty!

Squid taste with their tentacles.

There is a town in North Carolina called **"Boogertown."**

Chuckle!

MEGA FLUFFBALL!

Lucille the English Angora rabbit gets her long fur blow-dried by owner Charlie Lacey before a pet show in California.

Just a few more minutes, Lucille!

ZZZZ...

PEEK-A-BOO!

PYGMY SEAHORSE

MOTH

LEAF-TAILED GECKO

46

EASTERN SCREECH OWL

cooo-eee!

ASIAN HORNED FROG

47

FAMOUS FACES!

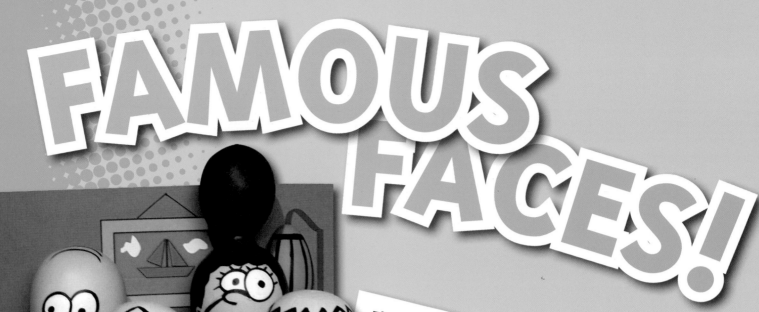

The Simpsons have been painted on eggs by American artist John Lamouranne. He used eggs for their heads, bodies, and even for Marge's hair.

The sounds made by Chewbacca in the Star Wars movies were actually moaning camels.

Homer Simpson's catchphrase "D'oh!" is so famous that it's in the dictionary.

A hot air balloon made in the shape of Darth Vader's mask was launched into the skies over Belgium—it was 85 feet high and 70 feet wide.

Every Doctor Who ever—all eleven of them—have been knitted by Allison Hoffman, from Austin, Texas. She made the dolls for her husband, a huge Doctor Who fan, and each one took five days.

There is a real asteroid between the planets Mars and Jupiter named TARDIS, after Doctor Who's time machine.

POLICE PUBLIC CALL BOX

FREE FOR USE OF PUBLIC

Shrek-mad fans Amanda Billington and Nathan Gibbs got married dressed as Princess Fiona and Shrek in England in 2013. Everybody else at the wedding had to dress up as well.

Errrr...

I hope this green paint washes off Nate?

The main voice actors in Shrek never actually met each other during the making of the movie.

SEE YOU!

Some spiders can walk on water.

Tarantulas deep fried with salt and garlic are a popular snack in Cambodia.

Some spiders are as large as a dinner plate!

Water spiders live underwater.

Some female spiders eat their male mates.

Jumping spiders can jump up to six times their own height.

The blood of a spider is light blue.

THE WORLD

Every minute of every day

6,000 lightning strikes

The Sun produces enough energy to power the world for 45 million years

256 **BABIES ARE BORN**

4,200 flaps of a hummingbird's **wings**

The International Space Station travels 287 miles

12,000 airplanes are in the sky

26 iPhones are sold

2 MILLION GOOGLE SEARCHES

IN 60 SECONDS

all of these things happen!

100 PEOPLE GET MARRIED

A blue whale's heart beats 10 times

4,500 McDonald's burgers eaten

5 EARTHQUAKES

280,000 stars are born

YOU BLINK ABOUT 20 TIMES (UNLESS YOU ARE ASLEEP)

124 cars are built

1 BILLION ANTS ARE BORN

YOUR HEART BEATS UP TO 110 TIMES

53

PLOP CAM!

When a TV company filmed a herd of elephants, they spied on them using "plopcam," a remote-controlled camera hidden inside fake elephant dung.

Plopcam!

Your nose can remember **1 trillion** different scents.

Real elephant poop can weigh up to 20 lb a plop!

Potato chips were invented by a **Mr. Crum.**

Promise?

Ants can survive a fall from any height.

If you ate too many carrots, you would turn orange.

The duckbilled platypus has no **STOMACH.**

I'm so hungry!

More Monopoly money is printed each year than real money!

BODY LONG BITS

Fingernail 39 inches
Melvin Boothe from the U.S.

Foot 18.5 inches
Robert Wadlow from the U.S.

Hands 12.2 inches
Leonid Stadnyk from Ukraine

Big toe 5 inches
Matthew McGrory from the U.S.

Nose 3.46 inches
Mehmet Ozyurek from Turkey

Eyelash 2.75 inches
Stuart Muller from the U.S.

Nick Stoeberl from Monterey, California, has a tongue that has been measured at an incredible

3.988 inches!

That's big enough to hold FIVE ring doughnuts!

ACTUAL SIZE!

BIG FOOT

This sneaker probably wouldn't fit you, because it's 18 feet long, and 10 feet high! That's about the size of an elephant, and U.S. shoe size 845!

GLOW FOR IT!

SCARY SCORPION

As if they weren't frightening enough, scorpions can glow in the dark! Their glow may help them to hunt in the darkness.

WEIRD RODENT

This little mouse has been bred to have glow-in-the-dark ears, feet, nose, and tail.

FLUORESCENT FUNGUS

Many types of mushrooms glow in the dark, but nobody really knows why!

BRIGHT EYE-DEER

Reindeer in Finland have their antlers sprayed with glowing paint to help people spot them in the dark!

GLOWING CAT

Scientists in South Korea have been able to make some cats glow in the dark.

OPEN WIDE

This glowing moray eel was photographed off the coast of the Philippines. They give a nasty bite and have been known to bite diver's fingers off!

INTO THE BLUE...

Blue whales measure 85 feet long and weigh up to 120 tons. That's the same as **24 elephants!**

Bottlenose dolphins recognize themselves in mirrors.

Whales and dolphins have accents.

Dolphins, whales, and porpoises do not chew their food. They swallow it whole!

Whales have enormous appetites. When a blue whale gulps a mouthful of food, it eats up to **half a million calories** —that's the same as 1,500 slices of chocolate cake!

YOUR BODY IN NUMBERS

You have roughly **100 BILLION** brain cells, called neurons.

You have around **3 TRILLION** pores (tiny holes) in your skin.

We lose around **60-100** hairs a day.

An adult makes around **3.5 pints of spit a day.** That's roughly 160 gallons a year!

There are **650** muscles in the human body. Your biggest muscle is in your backside.

THERE ARE

5 MILLION

hairs on the adult human body, on average
(some people are hairier than others).

You fart

14

times a day
on average.
This is likely
to go up if
you eat a lot
of beans!

Average number of breaths
taken by a human each day =

23,000,000

Average number of heartbeats a day =

100,000

That's 35 million a year.

The small and
large intestine
are around

26 feet

long in total in an
adult. They are curled
up in the stomach.

SAY HELLO

Bottle-opener

Old sink

Castle tower

Sniff... I've got a runny nose!

Hey, blockhead!

Watch it!

Your **EYEBROWS** regrow every 64 days.

TOTALLY LOCO

This train would be very hard to miss! Artist Olek, from Poland, covered an old steam locomotive in bright, multi-colored knitting.

It costs about **$50,000** to send a single pound of anything to the Moon.

Fleas can live **for a year** without eating.

YOU LOOKIN'

Match these animal eyes to their owners in the list below. Can you spot the odd one out?

Goat • Crocodile fish • Llama
Macaw • Horse • Elephant
Hornbill • Owl butterfly • Cat
Mossy frog • Lizard

11

1

5

8

7

10

AT ME?

SAY CHEESE!

The world's largest bat is the giant golden-crowned flying fox, which has a wingspan of 5–6 feet.

A single bat can eat more than 600 bugs in one hour. That's like a person eating 20 pizzas in an evening!

The smallest bat in the world is the Kitti's hog-nosed bat. It is about the size of a bumblebee and weighs less than a penny.

During the American Civil War, bat droppings were used to make gunpowder.

In China and Japan, bats are symbols of good fortune and happiness.

A photographer in Indonesia got lucky when he snapped this picture of a bat flying near his home—the little guy even appeared to smile for the camera!

DOG DAYS

Check out these moves!

Teka the four-year-old papillon spaniel is a sporting superstar. Her owners took her snowboarding and she loved it so much that they decided to try some other sports. Now she enjoys surfing and even flying under a bunch of balloons. That's one daring dog!

Surfing →

Snowboarding

Flying

woohoo!

Question time...

We asked Teka's owners, Jim and Amanda Holmdahl, all about their amazing dog.

Q How did you teach Teka these sports?

A Teka picks up new sports easily because when people are watching her she will do something over and over again. She loves the attention!

Q When and how did Teka learn to fly?

A She started flying in 2013—we trained her on a zip line between two tall trees.

Q What is Teka's favorite sport?

A Her favorite sport is chasing our two cats, and her second favorite is flying!

SPROUT OUT!

James Hutcheon eats Brussels sprouts every day! That's around 50,000 in his life so far.

How many types of Brussels sprouts are there? **21**

An amazing 38,813 sprouts have been squashed into this Mini! Lawrence Jones spent a day filling the car with them.

What did the world's heaviest sprout weigh?

18 pounds!

The sprouts in the car weighed the same as 29 reindeer! If laid out end to end, they would be a mile long.

How many Brussels sprouts could you eat in one minute?

The record is 31!

YH63 RZK

WHEELY COOL!

Septimus the tortoise is back on the move after having his front legs replaced with model airplane wheels. The 23-year-old pet had the surgery after being injured. He is now able to turn himself around and go backward, which he couldn't do before.

A praying mantis has just one ear, and it's on its stomach!

Whooosh!

AMAZING

Chicky the dolphin has learned how to paint! She holds a paintbrush in her mouth, and carefully paints colorful brush strokes on a canvas next to her pool.

A hippopotamus can run faster than a man.

SNAIL'S PACE

Hurry up!

This dozing frog couldn't be bothered to move when a slimy snail decided to slide over it. Being a snail, it took eight minutes to complete the move!

ANIMALS!

At birth, a baby kangaroo is smaller than a cherry.

COLD FEET?

This striking seabird is a blue-footed booby, named for (you guessed it!) its bright blue feet. The brighter the better, as females pick the males with the bluest feet to be their mate.

Tortoises in disguise

Tortoise lover Katie Bradley makes stylish clothing for these slow moving animals. The knitted designs, including a birthday cake and a hamburger, make the tortoises easier to see when they are walking across a lawn!

THE REINDEER

THE CHEESEBURGER

Oh, very funny!

THE CRAB

THE SHARK

Hey Bob, your back's on fire!

THE BIRTHDAY CAKE

DIVE! DIVE! DIVE!

Emperor penguins can dive 1,750 feet underwater—that's a third of a mile!

DAFT DWELLINGS

Excuse me, I'm looking for the old woman.

Holiday Cottage in New Zealand.

Basket-making Company in Newark, Ohio.

LONGABERGER

Spaceship home in Italy.

Old gas station in Zillah, Washington.

GAS

Fill 'er up please.

Milk and Sugar sir?

85

GANGNAM BEAR!

This wild brown bear cub was spotted showing off in front of his mom doing his best Gangnam Style dance!

Cockroaches have extra teeth in their stomachs.

Wearing pajamas in public is popular in Shanghai, China. They have "pajama police" to try to stop people doing it!

It wasn't me officer!

Humans shed nine pounds of skin each year!

PUMPKIN ART

Each Halloween, the "Great Jack O'Lantern Blaze" takes place at Van Cortlandt Manor, U.S.A. It features hand-carved pumpkins, built into giant models that are all lit up, such as this terrific triceratops.

The largest pumpkin pie ever baked was made in 2010 and weighed 3,699 pounds.

CRAZY DAYS!

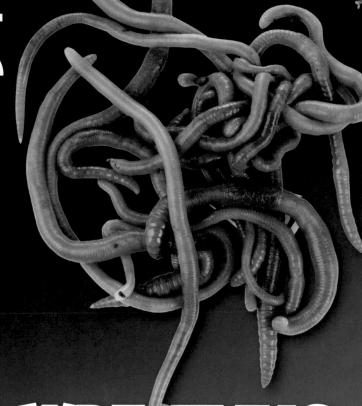

The annual U.K. **WORM CHARMING** festival sees competitors trying to tempt worms out of the ground. The record is 567!

THE WORLD TOE-WRESTLING CHAMPIONSHIPS
takes place in the U.K. in August.

On a special day each November **DOGS ARE WORSHIPPED** in Nepal, at the festival of Kukur Tihar.

At the Norwegian **Ice Music Festival** each February, musicians play instruments made out of ice.

La Tomatina is a giant

TOMATO THROWING

battle held in the Spanish town of Buñol every August.

Each February in Ivrea, Italy, thousands of townspeople get into nine teams to take part in the

Battle of the Oranges.

They throw the fruit at each other for three days!

The Christmas Tree-Throwing World Championships are held each year in Germany.

A village in Spain holds a

GOAT-TOSSING

festival in January, where a goat is thrown out of a church tower and caught, unharmed, by the crowd below.

International

Pillow Fight Day

takes place each April in cities across the world.

Too good to eat?

Breakfast food painting
by Prudence Staite

Chocolate sneaker
by Joost Goudriaan

Gummy bear chandelier
by YaYa Chou

Lion cake
by Steph Parker

Christmas dinner cake!
by Annabel de Vetten

WOOF WEDDING

Lucky pups Lanlan and Guaiguai got married at an animal rescue center in China. They each wore a special wedding outfit and were given a marriage certificate.

There are **3 CHICKENS** for every person on Earth.

PING!

An electric eel can produce enough power to run a **microwave.**

One day on Venus lasts for 117 Earth days.

LOST IN SPACE

NO WAY!

UNDERPANTS

Astronauts on the International Space Station fire their dirty underwear into space.

CAMERAS

Two cameras were dropped by astronauts on spacewalks, never to be seen again.

GOLF BALLS

Astronaut Alan Shepard hit two golf balls on the surface of the Moon—they traveled for miles!

TOOL BAG

A tool bag was dropped on a spacewalk—it traveled around Earth 4,000 times and was big enough to see with a telescope.

POOP

Astronaut poop is fired out into space and burns up in the Earth's atmosphere.

SPATULA

A spatula floated off into space when an astronaut used it to repair a space shuttle.

PLIERS

A pair of pliers disappeared into space from the space shuttle Discovery.

GARBAGE

Bags of garbage are thrown out of the International Space Station, but burn up before reaching Earth!

ASHES

The ashes of Gene Roddenberry, creator of the Star Trek TV series, were fired into space.

GLOVE

An astronaut's glove traveled at 17,500 mph around the Earth for a month before burning up in the atmosphere!

PEE

Astronauts pee is pumped out into space where it freezes.

Big mouth!

Whale sharks suck prey into their giant mouth, which is so big that this diver was almost sucked inside. Luckily they only eat tiny creatures—they would spit out a human!

Woah, stop creeping up on me!

They can hang beneath schools of fish and "vacuum" them up.

One whale shark was followed swimming around the Pacific Ocean—it swam 8,078 miles in 37 months!

The whale shark...

...lives for over 70 years.

...is the world's largest fish, growing to over 40 feet in length.

...has a mouth up to 5 feet wide, which contains around 350 rows of tiny teeth.

Each whale shark has a different pattern of spots on its back.

They have the thickest skin of any animal. It is 4 inches thick in some places.

LIGHT BITES

The world's first glow-in-the dark ice cream was eaten by British movie fans! They only found out it glowed when the lights went down!

Don't even think about it!

There's a town in Texas called Ding Dong.

Wedding cake was originally thrown at the bride.

Not even one?

There are no turkeys in Turkey.

A snail can have 25,000 teeth.

PENCIL PRECISION!

A mosquito has **47 TEETH.**

Check out this mini masterpiece! Hungarian sculptor Ágoston Birtalan carved these teeny-tiny chain links from the super-thin lead inside a pencil.

Each tiny link is hand-carved

There is a type of jellyfish that lives forever!

Your ears and nose **continue to grow** throughout your life.

Most frogs don't drink WATER.

Snowflakes can take as long as

one hour

to fall to the ground.

We are about one inch

TALLER

in the morning than we are in the evening.

Fluid in our joints builds up each night and adds to our height, but is squashed down during the day.

TOYBOY

Bess the cow-horned boxfish fell in love with a spiky plastic toy that was popped into her tank in Great Yarmouth, U.K. She thought her cute toy-boyfriend was a boxfish, too.

Say you feel the same way about me.

A slug's BOTTOM is behind its head.

Pardon?

There are 23 hours, 56 minutes and 4 seconds in a day, not 24 hours.

How high can a penguin jump out of water?

About six feet!

The smallest muscle in your body is in your ear.

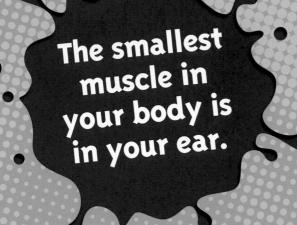

A man escaped a python's grip by biting its tail!

Chewing gum is illegal in Singapore.

Awww!

A group of pugs is called a GRUMBLE.

A giraffe can go without water longer than a camel can.

Until 1911, clocks in French railway stations were set five minutes fast SO people wouldn't miss their trains.

you bet!

Mel Blanc (the voice of Bugs Bunny) didn't like CARROTS!

Elephants suck their trunks like children suck their thumbs.

To have your photo taken with the first camera ever invented, you would have to sit still for eight hours!

Ice in the Antarctic is more than 2.5 miles thick in places.

Dogs and cats, like humans, are either right or left handed.

I still can't tell my right from my left though.

In Ancient Rome, people whitened their teeth using pee!

A bolt of lightning contains enough energy to toast

160,000

pieces of bread.

Unfortunately the bolt only lasts 1/10,000th of a second— so turning the bread over might be hard!

Missed again! Why cant we just get a toaster like everybody else?

BIG NUMBERS!

4

is the only number that has the same number of letters as the number itself

93,000,000 miles from the Earth to the Sun

180,497 islands in the world

16,000,000 pounds = weight of shrimp-like creatures (crustaceans) a blue whale eats each day

10,000,000,00

100,000,000,000,000 cells in your body

32 muscles in a cat's ear

44 squirts of a cow's udder makes 1 pint of milk

300 teeth in a great white shark's mouth

1,000,000,000 = approximate number of cars in the world

6,000,000,000 dust mites live in an average bed

jellyfish live in Jellyfish Lake, an island in Palau

20,000,000,000

7,000,000,000 = estimated population on Earth

0,000,000,000 insects thought to be alive at any moment

11 OUT OF EVERY **10** humans are left-handed

21,000,000 = approximate number of footsteps a person would take to walk around the Earth

Er, HOUSTON WE HAVE A PROBLEM!

Visitors to California's Coachella Music Festival were greeted by this giant floating astronaut. Measuring 57 feet high and 40 feet wide, the spaceman waved at the crowds as he passed by.

Mice can cough.

But you would need a microphone to hear it!

In France there's a place called Y

why?

Dinesh Shivnath Upadhyaya, from Mumbai, India, can fit

800 drinking straws

in his mouth at the same time!

IT'S NO YOKE!

Harriet the hen laid an egg that measured 9 inches all the way around!

A new kind of art called "eggcubism" has been invented by Dutch artist Enno de Kroon. Enno paints old egg cartons, and he calls this artwork Celebration.

Cats sleep for 70 percent of their lives.

Any good at math?

Er, why?

Two brown rats can multiply to **one million** rats in 18 months!

Hmm, more like "dribble!" I wish I had lips!

DIBBLE means to drink like a duck.

You can make a battery out of **lemons.**

− +

Queen bumblebees go **BALD** in old age.

A drop of ocean water takes 1,000 years to travel around the world.

All the pandas in the world belong to CHINA.

Grizzly bears can eat up to 90 pounds of food a day. That's equivalent to 360 quarter pounders from McDonald's.

MORE, MORE, MORE!

The Executive Yo-Yo

YO-YOS

Florida toy expert Lucky J. Meisenheimer owns over 6,000 yo-yos, the world's largest collection.

TANKS

Tank fan Andrew Baker, from England, has been collecting tanks for over 20 years and now has more than 80!

BATMAN

Batman clothes, backpacks, lunch boxes, posters, plates, bicycles, cups, garbage cans, stickers, candy, clocks, books, jewelry, perfume, and toothbrushes fill Chloe Konieczki's batcave-inspired bedroom in Illinois.

DOLLS

Mary Hickey from Ashbourne, Ireland, shares her home with around 420 dolls.

Horseshoe crabs have eyes on their tail.

We're pretty mixed up!

AN ADULT SPEAKS ABOUT 16,000 WORDS A DAY.

BIG NOSE WORLD CHAMPIONSHIPS
have been held every year since 1961 in Langenbruck, Germany!

We have about the same number of hairs on our body as a CHIMPANZEE.

There are about three million shipwrecks on the ocean floor.

Tropical velvet worms catch their insect prey with sticky ropes of slime squirted from their head.

Yeh, so think twice before you call me a hairy ape!

AWESOME EATERS!

GULP!

ADRIAN MORGAN ATE

20 BOILED EGGS

IN 84 SECONDS!

JAMIE "THE BEAR" McDONALD ATE

6.7 POUNDS OF ONION RINGS

IN 8 MINUTES!

SONYA THOMAS ATE

445 OYSTERS

IN 5 MINUTES!

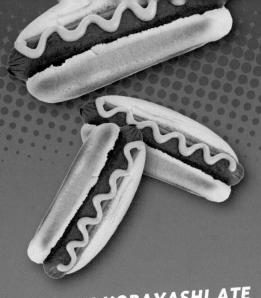

TAKERU KOBAYASHI ATE

110 HOT DOGS

IN 10 MINUTES!

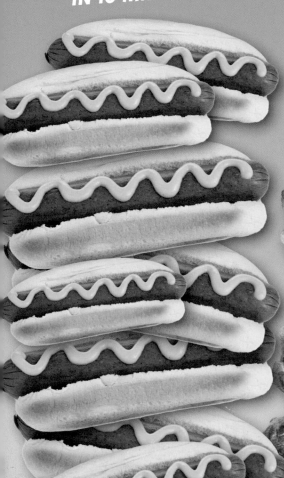

MOLLY SCHUYLER ATE A

72-OZ STEAK

IN 2 MINUTES, 44 SECONDS!

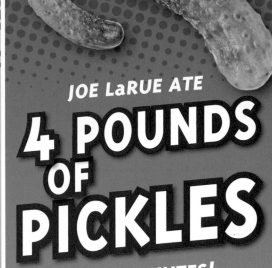

JOE LaRUE ATE

4 POUNDS OF PICKLES

IN 5 MINUTES!

ANT ATTACK!

Some worker ants have the job of taking the trash out of the nest and putting it in a "trash heap" outside.

Some birds put these ants in their feathers to get rid of tiny bugs that don't like the acid.

SNAIL FACE

Samuel Thuresson wanted to see how many snails he could fit on his face at the same time. Keeping very still, the brave eight-year-old managed 23 of the slimy creatures.

come on guys, let's crawl down his shirt!

Sloths move at just 0.15 mph.

...98, 99, 100. coming, ready or not!

Turnips turn GREEN when sunburned.

Crawfish signal to each other by peeing from a gland on their HEADS!

SLOW BOAT

Twenty men from Estonia managed to pull along a giant cruise ship that weighed 20,000 tons. Some of these mega-muscly men have also successfully pulled jet planes and trains!

Tom Sietas swam **656 FEET** underwater in one breath in 2008.

In 2011, James Roumeliotis spent 20 hours bouncing on a pogo stick—that's over **200,000** bounces!

French climber Alain "Spider-Man" Robert once climbed the 1,250-foot-high Empire State building—with no ropes.

Hungarian strongman Zsolt Sinka can pull a 50-ton Airbus 320 plane 100 feet—with his teeth!

Yeh, I tried it last year and I haven't been able to stand up since!

Benoît Lecomte swam **3,700 miles** across the Atlantic in 73 days.

ACKNOWLEDGMENTS

COVER © RZ Design – Shutterstock.com; **2** www.flyingdog.us; **3** © RZ Design – Shutterstock.com; **4** (t) © Lonely – Shutterstock.com, (l) © Alex Hubenov – Shutterstock.com, (r) © Dan Kosmayer – Shutterstock.com, (b) Shoe Bakery/Rex; **5** (t/r) © Jim Noetzel – Shutterstock.com, (t/l) Rex/Solent News, (c/r) © Guzel Studio – Shutterstock.com, (c/l) © Javier Brosch – Shutterstock.com, (b/l) Rex/Mohamed Babu/Solent News, (b/r) Rui Vieira/PA Wire/Press Association Images; **6** (t) © Lonely – Shutterstock.com, (l) © MSPhotographic – Shutterstock.com, (c) © Opas Chotiphantawanon – Shutterstock.com, (r) © Henrik Larsson – Shutterstock.com; **7** (l) © Nattilka – Shutterstock.com, (c) © FrameAngel – Shutterstock.com, (r) © Henrik Larsson – Shutterstock.com; **8** (b/l) © Eric Isselee – Shutterstock.com; **8–9** Jeff Cremer; **10** Uwe Anspach/DPA/Press Association Images; **11** (t) HAP/Quirky China News/Rex, (r/c, c, r/b) David Laferriere/Caters News; **14** Thanh Ha Bui/HotSpot Media; **15** (b) Arsgera – Shutterstock.com; **16** Rex/David Caird/Newspix; **17** (t) Rex/Andrew Tauber/Newspix, (b) Rex/David Caird/Newspix; **18–19** Rex/Brandon Goforth/Solent News; **20** (t) Lynne Cameron/PA Wire/Press Association Images, (b) Newsteam/SWNS.com; **21** (t) Martin Ellard/PA Archive/Press Association Images, (b) Rui Vieira/PA Archive/Press Association Images; **22–23** Rex/Mint Images; **24** (t) © Decha Chaiyarat – Shutterstock.com; **24–25** (b) Jun Kitagawa/ Rex; **26** (c) Reuters/Sukree Sukplang, (b) Rex/Richard Austin; **27** (t) Rex/Media Mode Pty Ltd, (c) Reuters/Stringer, (b) Noah Goodrich/Caters News; **28–29** Rex/Mohamed Babu/Solent News; **30–31** Shoe Bakery/Rex; **32** Imagine China; **33** Twin Design – Shutterstock.com; **34** (t) © Cultura/Photoshot, (b/l) Rex/Luka Esenko, (b/r) ThailandWildlife.com; **35** (t) Cassio Lopes/Caters News, (b/l) Michael Murphy, (r) Nick Garbutt/naturepl.com; **36–37** Nathan Edwards/Newspix/Rex; **38–39** Jeff Wright; **40** (t) © Borja Andreu – Shutterstock.com; **41** (c) © Volodymyr Krasyuk – Shutterstock.com, (b) © Ermolaev Alexander – Shutterstock.com; **42** (c) Rex/Andy Willsheer, (b) Getty Images; **43** (t) Dave Hersch/Rex, (c) Rainer Schimm/AP/Press Association Images, (b/r) Rex/Ross Hodgson; **44** (t) © Bob Orsillo – Shutterstock.com; **45** Glenn Fuentes/AP/Press Association Images; **46** (t/r) Mitsuhiko Imamori/Minden Pictures/FLPA, (t/l) Carrie Vonderhaar/Ocean Futures Society/National Geographic Creative, (b) Thomas Marent/Minden Pictures/FLPA; **47** (t/r) Gerrit Vyn/naturepl.com, (b) Thomas Marent/Minden Pictures/FLPA; **48** (t) Caters News, (b) Rex/Eye Ubiquitous; **49** (t) Allison Hoffman/Rex, (b) Rui Vieira/PA Wire/Press Association Images; **50–51** Rex/Colin Hutton/Bournemouth News; **52** (t/l) © Aaron Amat – Shutterstock.com; **54** John Downer Productions/naturepl.com; **55** (c) © schankz – Shutterstock.com, (b) © irin-k – Shutterstock.com; **56** (t) © Guzel Studio – Shutterstock.com; **57** Nick Stoeberl; **58–59** © Julian Stratenschulte/EPA/Corbis; **60** (t) Fabio Pupin/FLPA, (b/r) Suzi Eszterhas/Minden Pictures/FLPA, (b/l) © Dr. Charles Mazel/ Visuals Unlimited/Corbis; **61** (t/r) Choi Byung-kil/AP/Press Association Images, (l) Rex/Anne Ollila, (b/r) Alex Tyrrell/Caters News; **62–63** © pierre_j – Shutterstock.com; **66** (t/l) Aarriene Van Schoonhoven/Mercury Press, (t/r) Jay Joslin/Mercury Press, (b) Tom Oliver/Mercury Press; **67** (t/l) David Dunsmore/ Mercury Press, (t/r) Gini Reed/Mercury Press, (c/r) Tim Cordell/Mercury Press, (b) Steffen Kahl/Mercury Press; **68** (t) © Cameron Whitman – Shutterstock.com; **68–69** (b) Olek Studio; **69** (t) © Krasowit – Shutterstock.com; **70** (t/r) © Bildagentur Zoonar GmbH – Shutterstock.com, (c/l) © RedTC – Shutterstock.com, (c) © Sheli Jensen – Shutterstock.com, (c/r) © Aleksey Stemmer – Shutterstock.com, (b/l) © Eric Isselee – Shutterstock.com, (b/r) © NagyDodo – Shutterstock.com; **71** (t/l) Suren Manvelyan, (t/r) © Don Mammoser – Shutterstock.com, (c/r) © Robert Bagdi – Shutterstock.com, (b/l) © Liew Weng Keong – Shutterstock.com, (b/r) © Eric Isselee – Shutterstock.com; **72–73** Robertus Sudiatmokos/Solent N/Rex; **74–75** www.flyingdog.us; **76** Rex/M & Y News Ltd; **77** Rex/Mini; **78** (t/l) Rex/M & Y News Ltd, (t/r) © David Carillet – Shutterstock.com, (b/l) Caters News; **79** (t) Rex/Lessy Sebastian/Solent News, (c) © Nattika – Shutterstock.com, (b/r) © javaman – Shutterstock.com; **80–81** Rex/Solent News; **82–83** Getty Images; **84** (t) Caters News, (b) Rex/Sipa USA; **85** (t/l) Sipa Press/Rex, (sp) Getty Images; **86** Rex/Mark Sisson; **87** (b/l) © Pan Xunbin – Shutterstock.com, (r) © maximult – Shutterstock.com; **88** (t/l) © Jacek Fulawka – Shutterstock.com; **88–89** Bryan Haeffele; **90** (t/r) © Africa Studio – Shutterstock.com; **91** (t, b/l) © Picsfive – Shutterstock.com, (c/l) © Tim UR – Shutterstock.com, (b/r) © Neil Lockhart – Shutterstock.com; **92** Rex/Solent News; **93** (t/r) Mikey Jones / Caters News, (l,c) YaYa Chou, (b/r) Caters News; **94** Reuters/Stringer; **95** (t) © Valentina_S – Shutterstock.com, (c/r) © MrGarry – Shutterstock.com, (b/r) © alexokokok – Shutterstock.com; **96** (t) © Lonely – Shutterstock.com, (l) © nito – Shutterstock.com, (c) © stockphoto-graf – Shutterstock.com, (r) © FrameAngel – Shutterstock.com; **97** (l) © Horiyan – Shutterstock.com, (c) © maxim ibragimov – Shutterstock.com, (r) © Africa Studio – Shutterstock.com; **98–99** Mauricio Handler/Handlerphoto.com/Solent; **100** Rex/Anthony Upton; **101** (t/l) © Annkozar – Shutterstock.com, (b/r) © panbazil – Shutterstock.com; **102** (b) © leisuretime70 – Shutterstock.com; **102–103** (t) Rex/Agoston Birtalan; **104** (l) © Smit – Shutterstock.com; **105** Rex/Jeremy Durkin; **106** (t) © Aaron Amat – Shutterstock.com, (c/l) © ajt – Shutterstock.com, (b) © Kotomiti Okuma – Shutterstock.com; **107** (t) © cellistka – Shutterstock.com, (b) © xavier gallego morell – Shutterstock.com; **108–109** © NatUlrich – Shutterstock.com; **110** (t) © smuay – Shutterstock.com, (b) © Melinda Fawver – Shutterstock.com; **111** © Alex Hubenov – Shutterstock.com; **112** (t) © Norma Cornes – Shutterstock.com, (b) © Javier Brosch – Shutterstock.com; **113** © szpeti – Shutterstock.com; **116** AFP/Getty Images; **117** (b) © Neamov – Shutterstock.com; **118** Enno de Kroon; **119** (t) © Rumo – Shutterstock.com, (b) © Pakhnyushcha – Shutterstock.com; **120** (t/l) © Jennifer Sekerka – Shutterstock.com, (c/l) © Bahadir Yeniceri – Shutterstock.com, (c/r) © Ivaylo Ivanov – Shutterstock.com; **121** (b) © Eric Isselee – Shutterstock.com, (t/r) © gualtiero boffi – Shutterstock.com; **122** Rex/Zuma; **123** (t) Dan Rowlands/Caters News, (c) Chloe Konieczki, (b) Rex/Marc O'Sullivan; **124** © Suchatbky – Shutterstock.com; **125** © Eric Isselee – Shutterstock.com; **126** (t) © Lonely – Shutterstock.com, (l) © krichie – Shutterstock.com, anaken2012 – Shutterstock.com, (c) © Aaron Amat – Shutterstock.com, (r) © picturepartners – Shutterstock.com; **127** (l) © Dan Kosmayer – Shutterstock.com, (c) © Miguel Garcia Saavedra – Shutterstock.com, (r) © Africa Studio – Shutterstock.com; **128–129** Paul Quagliana/ Bournemouth News/Rex; **130** (t/r) You Touch Pix of EuToch – Shutterstock.com, (b) Marcus Palmgren/BLT/ Scanpix/TT News Agency/Press Association Images; **131** © Eric Isselee – Shutterstock.com; **132–133** AFP/Getty Images; **135** Dan Callister/Rex

Key: t = top, b = bottom, c = center, l = left, r = right, sp = single page

All other photos are from Ripley Entertainment Inc. and Shutterstock.com.
Every attempt has been made to acknowledge correctly and contact copyright holders and we apologize in advance for any unintentional errors or omissions, which will be corrected in future editions.

Check out more Fun Facts & Silly Stories!

some **clouds** weigh as much as **85 elephants...**

BOOK 1

FUN FACTS
RIPLEY'S
Believe It or Not!®
Kids
& SILLY STORIES

BOOK 2

FUN FACTS
RIPLEY'S
Believe It or Not!®
Kids
& SILLY STORIES

BOOK 3

FUN FACTS
RIPLEY'S
Believe It or Not!®
Kids
& SILLY STORIES

turtles can breathe through their **butts...**

If you have a fun fact
or silly story
why not email us at
bionresearch@ripleys.com